Tons Of Tongue Twisters
ISBN 978-1-7324180-7-3

Copyright 2024 by Mike Artell
All rights reserved

For more information or permissions, contact
www.mikeartell.com
MJA Creative, LLC

Tons Of Tongue Twisters

Tongue twisters are crazy fun. Some tongue twisters are easy to say ONE time but almost impossible to say three or more times. One of the most famous hard-to-say-three-times tongue twisters is, "TOY BOAT." The more times you say it, the more likely it is that you will say, "TOY BOYT."

Most of the tongue twisters in this book are like that; easy to say once, but much harder to say multiple times. Sometimes it's even harder to say the tongue twister just once but say it really FAST.

Are you ready to test your tongue twister talents?

TERRIFIC!!

LET'S GO!

The bad brats broke the bats.
The bad brats broke the bats.
The bad brats broke the bats.

Claude cracks crab claws.
Claude cracks crab claws.
Claude cracks crab claws.

Papa petted Pepper's puppy.

Willa wishes weird wishes.

**Fresh fried fish filets.
Fresher fried fish filets.
Freshest fried fish filets.**

Challenge:
How many times can you say this tongue twister in 10 seconds?

Silk socks stay silky soft.

Truck trunks.
Truck trunks.
Truck trunks.

CAN YOU SAY THIS ONE *FAST?*

Smelly cellars smell stale.

Popular pink play domes.
Popular purple play domes.

Extreme ice cream. Extreme ice cream. Extreme ice cream.

Creamed green beans.

Steve skied, skinned his knees, and sneezed on his sleeve.

Cheek-to-cheek.
Cheek-to-cheek.
Cheek-to-cheek.

Shad let Sid store his sled in his sled shed.

The clock ticked,
the clock tocked,
the clock tick-tocked.

The five guys tried to hide the fried pies.

The thicker stickers stick quicker than the slicker stickers.

**The fellow
with the cello
ate the mellow
marshmallow.**

Jack stacked the snack in the kayak.

Six strong safes.

Can you say it fast 3 times?

Carrie carried Harry's hairy canary.

Can you say it BACKWARDS fast 3 times?

French bread bakers
bake fresh French bread.
French bread bakers
bake fresh French bread.
French bread bakers
bake fresh French bread.

Austin ordered eight oysters.
All eight oysters Austin
ordered were awesome.

Tanya trains tarantulas two at a time in a tiny Texas town.

Tim tickled Tammy's toes Tuesday. Tammy tickled Tim's toes Thursday. Tim and Tammy are tremendous toe-ticklers.

Brian brought broad boards to build the boardwalk.

Michelle mashed mosquitoes, making a messy mosquito mush.

Danielle didn't drip-dry Drake's drapes.

A proud porpoise papa.

Steven's stained strainer was stranger than the stained strainer Steph saw.

"Look, Lauren! Lots of little lizards with little lizard legs!"

Challenge: How many times can you say this tongue twister in 10 seconds? GO!

Gross Ghosts.

CAN YOU SAY IT *FAST?*

Creepy crawly crocodiles carefully crunched crispy crunchy cracker crumbs.

Sherry sanded seven shelves.
Sherry sanded seven shelves.
Sherry sanded seven shelves.

Brian bought blue balloons, but Brianna brought the blue balloons back.

The bright blue boots belong in the broken boot box.

The coach was concerned that the catcher couldn't catch the curve. The catcher caught the curve! "Congratulations!" coach cried.

Phillip flipped flapjacks. Phillip's fancy flapjack flipping fascinated Phillip's friends.

Big black barges bumped bayou bridges.

Woodrow robbed Rowan while Rowan whittled wood.

Thistle trees have thick trunks. These three trees are thick-trunk thistle trees.

Wayne went to work as a white rice wrapper. He wrapped white rice really well.

**Rear wheel rims.
Rear wheel rims.
Rear wheel rims.**

Tommy thought tapping was tough. Tammy and Timmy took turns teaching Tommy to tap. Today, Tommy is a tip-top tapper.

Troy tried tying two tires together.

Cooper cleaned cuckoo clocks.

Dirk drained dirty ditches daily.

Every egret eats insects,
even evil egrets.

Cheerleaders lead cheers. The cheers the cheerleaders lead, lead the cheerers to cheer.

Peter planted purple peanut plants in his peanut patch. The peanut plants Peter planted produced purple peanuts. Peter politely peeled the peanuts for people who purchased the popular purple produce.

Four foolish florists flew to Florida.

Fresh flowers.
Fresher flowers.
Freshest flowers.

Here's a skillet.
Fill it with millet
and don't spill it.

Sometimes Stu sells shiny shoe soles by the shoe store.

Luscious lip-licking licorice.

Challenge: How many times can you say this tongue twister in 10 seconds? **GO!**

Five fat flies flew fast.

The truck struck the duck that was stuck in the muck.

Cara can clean clams, but Cara can't cook clams.

Harry had headaches. His hat hurt his head. "Help!" Harry howled. "Hand that hat here!" Heidi hollered.

Keeping cola cans in a cooler keeps the canned colas cool.

Howard's horses happily helped Heather's hens haul henhouses.

Can you say these tongue twisters three times <u>fast</u>? Do all three. **GO!**

Hippos hiccup.

Bats bit Brad's back.

The two taco tasters took turns tasting tacos.

Hannah handed Harvey her horsehair headband.

Hunter is a hurricane hunter. Hunter hunts hurricanes. Hurricane hunters have to hurry.

Colin clapped when Cora cut the coconut.

Chuck's children chewed cheese and chased Chuck's chickens.

    Warren rolled warm rolls.
    Warren rolled warm rolls.
    Warren rolled warm rolls.

Grace greased Reese's racer.
Grace greased Reese's racer.
Grace greased Reese's racer.

Clever clowns wear crystal crowns.

Sal was a skillful sailor. Several salty sailors stood still to see Sal sail. "That's some skillful sailing," the salty sailors said.

Wednesday, Wendell went to rent a winch. Winston already rented the winch Wendell wanted to rent. "Waaaa! Why did Winston rent that winch?" Wendell whined.

A pair of pears disappeared after Peter Pearson appeared near the place where the pears were placed.

Slippery, sloppy ski slopes.
Slippery, sloppy ski slopes.
Slippery, sloppy ski slopes.

Can you say it 3 X FAST?
GO!

Several silly sheep slept silently.
Several silly sheep slept silently.
Several silly sheep slept silently.

Steven Simon saw six stray steers sitting still.

Was the wire rope wet when Wyatt wrapped it?

Kip was a cliff-climber.
Kip was careful.
Kip was cautious.
Kip was a careful, cautious cliff-climber.

Fred's friend Phil faithfully flew the flag.

Priscilla's sister painted Patricia's puppy's paws.

The paper proclamations the proud prince preferred printing were parchment paper proclamations.

William Wright was a writer. William Wright had a right to write, but William Wright's writings were rarely right. What Willaim Wright wrote was really wrong.

Penny planned to purchase pretty pink and purple pom-poms.

Paul picked pits from prunes.
Paul was a prune-pit picking pro.

Seal skin, shark skin, sheep skin.
Seal skin, shark skin, sheep skin.
Seal skin, shark skin, sheep skin.

Bridgett's brother Blake built a brick bridge by the boulders beneath the bluffs.

Sly was shy, but when he spied the pigs in the pigsty, he plotted to pilfer the pigs on the sly. But the pigs were too sly for Sly. They slipped and slid in the slop until Sly tried another sty.

Steve eats steamed beets. Some beets Steve eats leave stains on Steve's sleeves. It seems silly, but Steve still says steamed beets beat unsteamed beets.

Conner's laptop is apt to topple if Conner keeps it atop the counter.

Portia's parents' party is probably on the pretty pink patio.

Doggone it, Dustin! You didn't dust the dirt from the dusty drapes.

Sybil's thimbles are simple thimbles.

Pearl picked a plaid purse.
The plaid purse is Pearl's purse.

The big-bellied boys
belched boldly.

Chip couldn't chop chocolate chips, so Chip chose to chop cherries.

Peter packed his puffed pastry with pickled pimento pudding.

The crooks couldn't catch the caravan of caramel-colored camels carrying cargo.

**Please pet
your porcupine properly.
Poor porcupine petting
produces porcupine pouting.
Porcupines prefer
proper petting.**

Lester said he lost the list, but I think Lester left the list in the loft.

Tory traded train tickets to Tucson to Taylor for ten tacos.

Brian Boyle brought broiled burgers to breakfast.

Carter cleaned out the cluttered coat closet.

This stew is super! It's super stew. Save Stu some.

Please promptly put Plato's pretty potted poppies in the plastic pots.

        Ostrich nostrils.
        Ostrich nostrils.
        Ostrich nostrils.

Was who you're with where you are with you when you were where you were?

Wanda Riggs wears weird wigs.
What weird wigs Wanda wears!

Please pass the plastic plates.

Jerry's jealous of his cherry jelly. Jerry's cherry jelly isn't jelly that Jerry shares.

Britt is building a brick building.

Tim's thin, but Tim's twin is thin too.

> Let's let Luke loose.
> Let's let Luke loose.
> Let's let Luke loose.

Can you say it 3 X FAST?
GO!

**Cracked corks.
Cracked corks.
Cracked corks.**

Say it FAST!!

Thor's thumb is sore from throwing swords.

Five friendly frogs fed on fat flies.

The sweet, sticky syrup stains on Sergei's shirt were similar to the sweet, sticky syrup stains on his sister Sadie's shirt.

Mixing mustard is messy, and mustard mixers are master mess-makers. Major messes are what mustard mixers make.

There are four floors. The fourth floor is the floral fixture floor. The floral fixtures are flawless.

Stacey Street tried tasting the tasty treat.

Paolo plowed the pasture prior to planting peanuts.

Lou's loops are loose loops.

Shannon shut some shutters, but she didn't shut other shutters. The sun will surely shine through the shutters Shannon didn't shut.

Is the loose goose Sue's goose or Lou's goose?

Would you rather wet weather or would you rather weather that wasn't wet?

Florence fixed the faulty faucets for Fiona.

Blair brought a bad pair of plaid pants.

One wombat won't walk, and one wombat won't run.

> **Quincy crushed a crate of creamed corn.**
> **Quincy crushed a crate of creamed corn.**
> **Quincy crushed a crate of creamed corn.**

Two tired tourists took turns touring Turkey.

Matt is a math master. Matt has mastered math.

Shawn sawed a short stick.
Shawn sawed a short stick.
Shawn sawed a short stick.

Professor P. Patrick Porter propelled the paddleboat by properly pressing the pedals.

Sue's shoes are sure soiled.

No one he knew knew
that he knew what he knew.
It was news to those he knew.

Wes Werner went West to work as a wrestler.

Some soap seems slippery.
Some soap seems solid.
Some soap seems slimy.
Some soap seems slick.

If the typing is terrible then the typists are too tired to type.

The sloppy stacks of slacks are slacks that Sally stacked.

There are three treats.
The three treats are free treats.

The carport collapsed, crushing the corrugated cardboard carton.

Henry Hickock hiccupped.
Henry Hickock hiccupped.
Henry Hickock hiccupped.

Noel never loaned Neville a long yellow ladder.

A couple of careful carpet cutters carefully cut the cantaloupe-colored carpet.

Ike Hill is a hill hiker.
Ike Hill likes to hike hills.

The shortstop stopped short.
The shortstop stopped short.
The shortstop stopped short.

How many hounds does Hannah have? Hannah has a hundred hounds that help Hannah hunt.

Big branch, bigger branch, biggest branch.
Big branch, bigger branch, biggest branch.
Big branch, bigger branch, biggest branch.

Several shoppers stopped to shop for slippers.

Shirley seems sure the Northshore shore is shorter than the Southshore shore.

It's bad to brag, but
Brad B. Becker
is a big bragger.

The scarecrow scares crows.

Is that the chest Chet checked?

Falcons' feathers flap fast. They're fast-flapping falcon feathers.

Pete's plans are plain because Pete prefers plain plans.

Sherman shops for shirts at the shirt shop and for shorts at the short shop.

Slippery shellfish shells slowly slam shut.

How will hollow-handled hooks help?

Say it FAST!

Flat flimsy foil.

Flat flimsy foil.

Flat flimsy foil.

Wes Wilson wants winter weather with wicked wild winds.

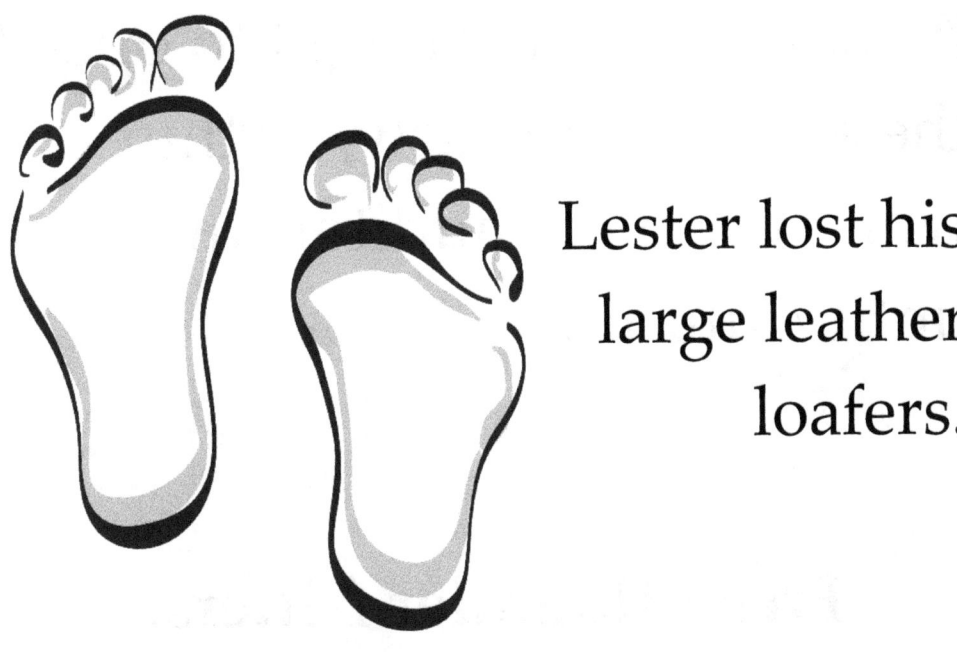

Lester lost his large leather loafers.

Paula perched her parrot on the pretty plastic plant.

She sold cool shirts and school skirts.

Although Arthur ought to open the auditorium early, Arthur won't open the auditorium until Autumn.

Fresh flounder fritters.
Fresh flounder fritters.
Fresh flounder fritters.

(Try saying this FAST!)

Which dishwasher washed which dish?

Pretty pendants make pretty party presents.

Two tortoises took turns tossing toasted tortillas.

Steph thought she thawed the steak, but she thawed the stew.

Is the left life raft the right life raft, or is the right life raft the right life raft?

How loud does a bloodhound howl when a bloodhound howls out loud?

Please put your pens, pencils, papers and posters in the proper place.

Reed writes well and Will reads well.

Chip stuck the chopsticks in the chips. Stop sticking the chopsticks in the chips, Chip!

Scarlett saw some Scottish soccer stars.

One wombat walked well while one wombat wobbled wildly.

Avril's ears ache and Arvel's ankles ache.

Colin couldn't clip the cat's claws and Kate could, so Kate clipped the claws. The clipped claws are the claws that Kate clipped.

Heath's seat is heated. The heat from Heath's heater heats Heath's seat.

Suzie says that CeCe got a "C" on the essay that Sissy saw.

Sheila is a sports reporter. She supposedly supports sports, but Sheila's sports reports are poor reports.

Fifty-four fire fighters fitfully fought the fire.

Ben Baker had baked beans and bread for breakfast. It was a bread-and-bean breakfast. Ben boasted that the bread-and-bean breakfast was the best.

Fred frowned at Frank who frowned at Phil. Then Fred, Frank, and Phil frowned at the fellow who forgot the French fries.

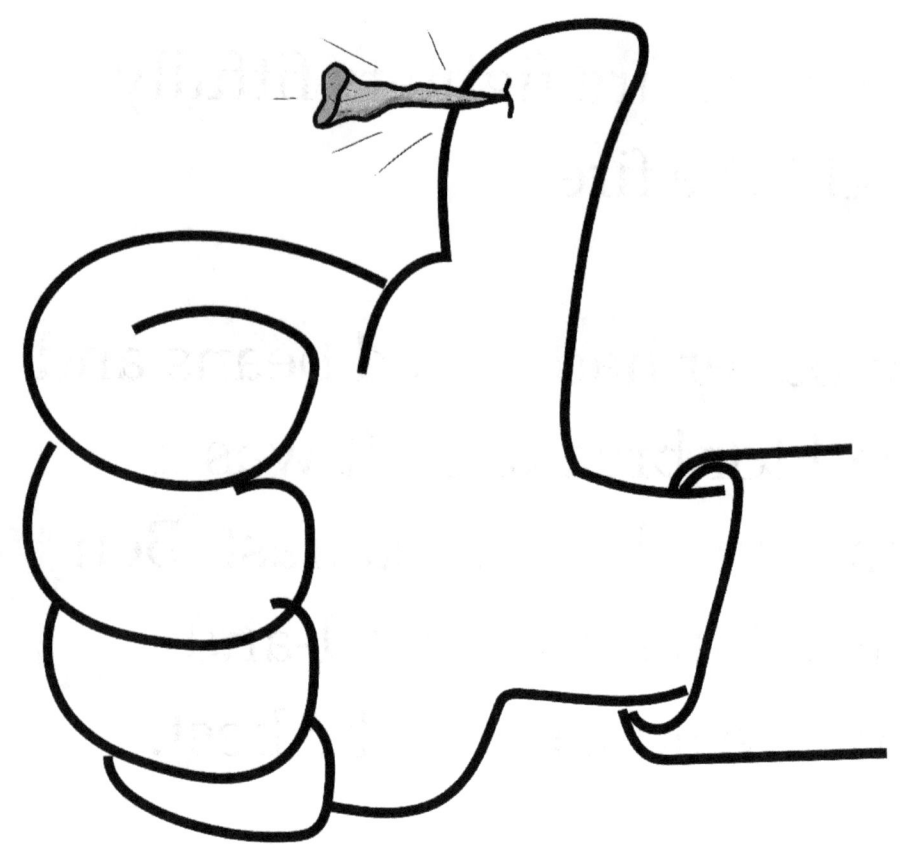

Stella's thumb is sore. I see a thorn stuck in Stella's thumb. It's a sore thumb thanks to the sticky thorn.

Can you say each one 3 X FAST?

GO!

Blaine bought blackboards. The blackboards Blaine bought were blank.

Chauncey checked the chalk. Chauncey was a chalk-checker.

Check your change, Jane. Is it the same as Shane's change?

Hilda held the halter as an elder helped her hold her horse.

The bugs buzzed and bugged Buzz.

A kitty
in the city bit a kiddie…
what a pity!

EEEWWWW!!!

You put your stinky pinky in my drinky!

Were the woods where Woody was redwood woods or whitewood woods?

Ruth's youths are uncouth youths. The uncouth youths are Ruth's.

Unpack the snacks in the backpacks and put them in stacks in the back of the backpack shack.

The street sweepers sweep steep streets. The street sweepers sweep steep streets. The street sweepers sweep steep streets.

Dee is sleeping deeply. Dee is a deep sleeper. The deeper Dee sleeps, the sleepier Dee seems.

Bo Peep broke both feet.
Bo Peep broke both feet.
Bo Peep broke both feet.

See the sheep sleep? They are sleepy sheep.

The bowlers brought bluish-black bowling balls.

Chad sold the cheap cherry chair to Chelsea who sold the chunky chest to Chuck.

 When Drew draws doodles, Drew dawdles.

This sink stinks. It's a stinky sink.

Chubby chimps chase shrimps.

She said she's sad. She's sad she said.

Jack tracked the crushed cracker crumbs to a truck of crackers.

Brett's bank is the branch bank. Brett banks at the branch.

 The winding road was wet. It was a really wet, winding road.

Two junky dump trucks just dumped junk at the junction.

The road workers rode to work to work on the road.

Nancy's Auntie isn't her nanny. She's her Auntie not her nanny.

Steve snickered as several sick, sneezy snails sailed south.

Did the tall troll throw the toad through the toll tunnel?

When Wanda West runs, Wanda won't rest.

Four furry ferret feet full of fat fleas.
Four furry ferret feet full of fat fleas.
Four furry ferret feet full of fat fleas.

This soup is soapy. Someone slipped soap into the soup.

A tree toad with three toes is a three-toed tree toad.

Chester just suggested that Justin is just a jester.

Sarah saw a stegosaurus stealing steel saws.
"Stop stealing!" Sarah shouted. "Say you're sorry."
"So sorry," the shy, saw-stealing stegosaurus sighed.

Percy was a pickle picker and packer. He picked and packed pickles perfectly and was promoted to Professional Pickle Picker and Packer. Percy proved that Professional Pickle-Pickers and Packers can pick and pack pickles properly.

Proud peacocks playfully pecked platypuses.

Hedda hit her hardhat hard however her head hardly hurt.

Misha misses mushing in Michigan. Mushing is a "must" for Misha.

Warren's armor was warm because Warren wore an armor warmer.

The pilot put a pair of plastic pliers in the plane.

Clear, cool cola in clean cool cans.
Clear, cool cola in clean cool cans.
Clear, cool cola in clean cool cans.

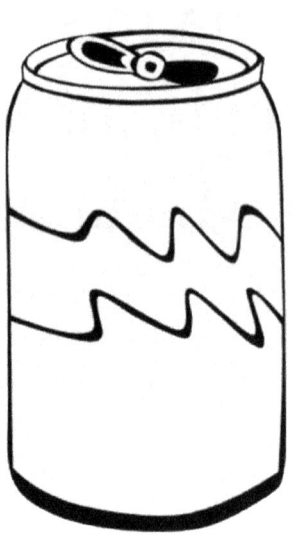

A kid caught a cold from a calico kitty cat.
A kid caught a cold from a calico kitty cat.
A kid caught a cold from a calico kitty cat.

I think **those** sticky thistles are thicker than **these** sticky thistles.

Pat Figg put the fat pig
by the fig patch.
Pat Figg put the fat pig
by the fig patch.
Pat Figg put the fat pig
by the fig patch.

*Say each of these one time as **FAST** as you can!*

The better batters in baseball bat boldly.

The gate guard wore guard garb.

Silvia saw six soft, silk slippers.

That man grows mangoes by the mangroves.

Six singers sang several songs softly. The songs the singers sang sounded sweet.

The elves helped the ill elk.

The cook cooked the corn in copper cooking kettles because copper cooking kettles cook corn quickly.

Wilma warned Warren about the worn wire.

Tula took the two torn tutus to the tutu tailor.

Tori tickled the tired ticket-taker.

The coffee in the cup is creamy 'cause the coffee contains coffee creamer.

Papa Porter purchased a pack of peppered pickles. If Papa Porter purchased a pack of peppered pickles, then where's the peppered pickle package Papa Porter purchased?

I thought he started to sort the salted sauces, but the sauces are still unsorted.

Braydon bragged about the bag of bones. It was a big bag of broken bones.

The silent street sweeper swept the streets while slumbering sleepers snored.

Luke's lizard looks lazy.

Z-z-z-z-z

That's a lazy lizard, Luke.

Kenny the candy canner can't can a can of candy, can he?

Sal slipped and lost the silver, slotted sauce spoon.

A pair of pants.
A pair of plaid pants.
A pair of purple plaid pants.

Wanda watched the runners run by. One by one, Wanda watched them run.

Ditch diggers dig ditches.
Ditch diggers dig ditches.
Ditch diggers dig ditches.

I have a heifer with half a hoof. Have you ever had a half-hoof heifer?

Savannah ate a banana in a cabana in Havana.

Brooke brought both books.

Norton gnaws noodles. Norton is a noodle-gnawer. Nobody gnaws noodles like Norton.

Emma's Mama and Emma's Maw-Maw made Emma a muumuu.

Andy owns the only iron anchor on the island and that angers Anders.

Wet, round rings.
Wet, round rings.
Wet, round rings.

Although it took extra effort for Tex to exit, Tex exited excellently.

Frances fancies frilly flowers.

Wait! This isn't the end of this book. Would you like to write YOUR OWN original tongue twisters? If so, keep reading…

YOU CAN WRITE YOUR OWN TONGUE TWISTERS!

Tongue twisters are fun to SAY, but they're super fun to WRITE! Would you like to write your own original tongue twisters? Here's one way to do it:

Step 1. Think of someone's name that starts with two consonants. Some examples would include FR, CH, and ST. Some examples of names that begin with FR include Freddy,

Frances, Frankie, and Francesca. CH names include Charlie, Chelsea, Chanda, and Chandler. ST names include Stephanie, Stacey, Stormy, and Stella. You can probably think of a lot more.

Step 2. Let's say you decide to us a name that starts with FR – like, FREDDY. Write that name.

Step 3. Now comes the fun part. Try to make a sentence by starting with the name and adding some additional words.

First, add another FR word. After you do that, mix it up! Start with an F but add words that have a different second letter. The second letter can be a consonant or a vowel. Here's an example:

FReddy FRied Fish.

Keep going…

FReddy FRied FLying FIsh.

Add more words and give Freddy a second name:

FReddy FOrman FRied FIve FLying FIsh FRiday.

You can keep adding words until you like the way your tongue twister sounds.

Give it a try.

Good luck!

About the author

Mike Artell has written and illustrated tons of books. You can find his books in bookstores and online at all the major bookseller sites.

Mike has shared his wordplay and cartooning techniques at many educational and literacy conferences, and he has visited more than 1,000 schools across the United States, Europe, and Asia where he helps kids (and their teachers!) learn to think, write, and draw more creatively.

You can find more information
about Mike Artell's books,
school and library visits and
conference presentations at
www.mikeartell.com
and on social media.

www.ingramcontent.com/pod-product-compliance
Lightning Source LLC
Chambersburg PA
CBHW071856160426
43209CB00005B/1081